Lasting
Impressions

Lasting Impressions

All Original Lines & Poems
For
Cards & Scrapbooking

PHALLE MARIE WRIGHT

authorHOUSE®

AuthorHouse™
1663 Liberty Drive
Bloomington, IN 47403
www.authorhouse.com
Phone: 1-800-839-8640

Edited by Amanda Snyder & Charity Frie.

Illustrations by grandchildren: Sydnie Jo, Gillian Marie & Douglas John Frie, Kalvin Otto & Karmin Olivia Wright, Madison Irene & Melanie Marie Monroe.

Published by AuthorHouse   02/27/2012

ISBN: 978-1-4685-4976-8 (sc)
ISBN: 978-1-4685-4975-1 (e)

With kind heart and thankfulness
this book is dedicated
to
my family and friends—
from where my inspiration was born.

Contents

Family

A family weaves the newest roots
tenderly amongst the old
with strength and love to guide their way.

᠀᠊᠊᠀

Tis Written
Tis written, every chapter and verse,
a story within us unheard,
save the ones that we love most,
give voice to every word.

᠀᠊᠊᠀

Within family
Within family
one's second self is found—
centered around
love that gives us strength.

Sydnie

Images
Come, let us sit close beside each other
and for the camera sweetly smile.
Let us hold fast to memories past
and dance with them for awhile.

Home

Welcome home and to all the comforts within.

❧☙

Plenty and grace be to this place.

❧☙

Let the one's who tarry, linger still.

❧☙

Come mingle here and welcome be.

❧☙

Welcome
Welcome to our home
where hearts are eased with laughter
and wayward wrath doth fall.
Come weave for us a memory,
we welcome one and all!

Follow Your Heart

Follow your heart home this season,
not necessarily the place you were born and raised
or the place that you call home now.
It is the place that calls out to you—
a tugging in your chest,
the yearning to just lay down your soul and rest.
Let tranquility wash over you
and share its peaceful ride,
and you will know the meaning of *Home* is found,
down deep in each of us, inside.

Beyond the Front Door

The talk at the table,
the slam of the door,
the echo of laughter
rumbles on the floor.

Peeps around the corner,
the light in the hall,
hiding places often found
markings on the wall.

The drip of the faucet,
toothpaste in the sink,
losing soap in the tub
from mom a subtle wink.

The guiding advice from father,
boundary's gone awry,
the riddles we told
a tolerant look in his eye.

The melody of the daytime,
the sigh in the still of the night,
magical bedtime stories told
pulling the covers up tight.

Oh the savory scent of home
where memories return
of youth and love
and all we grew to learn.

<u>Home</u>
I long to go back
to the house upon the hill
where the laughter sang,
the good times rang,
and the memories always will.
Sometimes I forget
it's someone else's home now,
with another's song,
it's not really wrong,
it just doesn't seem right somehow.
Part of me is still there,
memories don't fade with years
of childhood dreams,
the house still seems,
security for all my fears.

Love

May this day be as dear to you
as you are to my heart.

❧❦

I thought my heart
was standing room only
before you walked in.

❧❦

I sit here and try to think
of all the ways and reasons I love you,
and all I can do is smile.

❧❦

The comfort of you encircles my heart
and curls up within my sigh.

❧❦

I have your essence folded within my heart
and every now and then I take it out and add a star.

❧❦

It's like you turn on a hundred blinking Christmas lights
inside my body.

His/her smile follows her/him,
you can almost see the heartstrings.

❧ ❦

Saving Grace
My song was all out of tune
and like an angel composing on a harp,
you gently strummed on the strings of my heart
until I found harmony again.

❧ ❦

If I lay your hand upon my chest
would you feel my heart fall
each time I look into your eyes?

❧ ❦

And like the well worn path under a child's swing,
you have left your mark in my heart.

❧ ❦

Through It All
Through all the seasons we have shared
and all the sorrows we have faired,
through all the memories we have made
and all our hopes that never fade,
I have loved you so very much.

Sydnie

Interludes

Nightfall comes and my dreams
are filled with romantic interludes with you.
Of songs we've yet to sing
and words we've yet to say,
the joys of our tomorrows
and memories of yesterdays.
So sleep softly, my love,
for the nights bring love anew,
forever yours, forever true.

જે≪

May You Dream Tonight

May you dream tonight
of familiar faces and comfortable places,
and when tomorrow comes,
although we are apart,
may you feel the loving arms that hold you
deep within my heart.

જે≪

Always, There is a Window

Always, there is a window
that beckons me when you are away,
and it matters not what road you're on,
what path you take or how long you're gone,
for you are always in my heart.

Missing You

My eyes are filled with rain,
it gently trickles down my face.
Sadness comes when you are gone
and I'm in an empty space.
My heart feels so lonely,
but patiently I wait for you,
knowing your smile, your sweet embrace
will again our love renew.

Father

Mom Told Me
Mom told me how you held her hand
when I was born
and how you would rescue me
from her weary arms
in the middle of the night.
She told me
how you would talk to me about life
when I was still a wee babe,
and later when I grew a little
whirl me around in the air
until I saw stars.
And I just wanted to thank you
for all the stars I ever saw
in your eyes.

స్ళ

I find myself studying him
for I find in his strength to be
strength in me.

స్ళ

Breakfast
What forces led me to your side
to sit with you in the quiet of the day?
So many early mornings we shared,
your coffee growing cold
as I was growing strong.

Peanut Butter Sandwiches

"Get out the peanut butter
and a knife," you said.
"Now gently paint with it,
just one slice of bread."
Together we folded our bread to their edges
and into each our own glass of ice cold milk,
dunked our adolescence.
Said you, "Gotta wait a bit,
until it is just right . . .
soaked up through and through
before you take a bite.
And once you get it inside,
swirl it all about.
Try hard not to smile
or it'll come dribbling out."
We both tried to hold our excitement
as we swirled our tongues around,
attempting to keep the peanut butter
from sticking to the roof of our mouths.
You looked at me, and I at you,
as the goodness came dribbling out.

Husband

New Girl in Town

Sometimes you treat me
like the new girl in town,
and come hanging around,
bathing me in sunshine
for want of my smile,
and as I embrace
your all-grinned face,
I can't help but smile too.

❧❧

My Dearest

As natural as the sun rises
giving new light to the day,
you enter my soul
and chase away
shadows
that hide within.
And as the breath of spring
nurtures the earth,
your caress softly says
there is always room
to begin, to grow, to be.
As we face this world together now,
just we
you and me
let's travel together
growing ever closer
until we
just can't bear to be
without each other.

A Day Complete

Late at night we lay in bed
after the kids are asleep,
deep down under the covers
our toes wiggle and meet.
This my love,
is what makes my day complete.

❧✦

Each Year

Each year we've spent together
we've experienced something new
through bold spirit and heart of grace,
hand in hand we've come shining through.

❧✦

My love is bound
with memories found
on the pages of our lives.

Mother

<u>Whenever I Think of You</u>
I think back to when my memory begins,
in your arms I slept,
your gentle touch lingering on,
begging to assure me
no harm would ever come.
And then I think of the laughter you bring
and the knowledge that you share.
I know somehow I need not worry
for you will always be there.
To hold me when I am lonely
and comfort me when I'm sad,
or squeeze just to celebrate
one of the many good times we've had.

❧◈

<u>Mom</u>
In treasured moments that we share
between the laughter and tears, somewhere
your comforting hand reaches out to say,
"I love you child, in every way."
A hand that taught me how to play,
preparing me for a later day,
to cook, and stitch, and gently be
the kind of mother you've been to me.

Seasoned With Love
I reach for the iron skillet
that once belonged to you
and days of my childhood come to life.
Tall birthday cakes
decorated prettier than the ones
in bakery windows,
catching the run away drips of frosting
with my tongue,
pancakes hot off the griddle,
rice pudding with big plump raisins
on a cold winter's day,
milk toast when the weather
got the better of me,
the shiny copper-bottomed pans
welcoming everyone
that came through the door,
and always another plate set at the table
when unexpected guests arrived.
Your special touch seasoned the meals,
prepared to perfection in this old iron skillet.
And now, with pride,
I serve my family from this skillet,
full of all the love and seasoning you gave to me.

The Apron

She pulls her duty-filled apron up over her head
now that the day is done.
Early morn found it crisp and clean
but now on its own hook tis hung.
Its starch given way to the trials of the day
along with the triumphs and sorrows,
all tucked within a hankie that's been
cradled in the pocket.
And tomorrow's on the horizon
and surely bound to bring,
the hugs and tugs of a toddler
grasping an apron string.

ॐॐ

The Dress

(Any color or style dress could be substituted here.)
Remember the red and white striped dress
you used to wear when I was very young?
I remember it hung in your closet for years,
and even after it no longer fit,
somehow it still belonged there.
I used to go in and just look at it,
all the smiles and heart songs
and the feeling of content
came streaming down in that gathered skirt
and wrapped around me.
I remember the comfort I found there
knowing that you were with me
all along the way.
You are so very special, you know,
for come rain or shine
I know you are beside me,
and will always be
all along the way.

Children/General

Sing with your children
so they will learn
how to live in harmony with all voices.

All cuddled up
neatly tucked within a dream,
a little angel at rest.

❧❧❧

My little sprout in the garden of stars
I wonder which light your dreams reach out to tonight.

Born Again

With you i am born again, for through your eyes
i see life in a candles shimmering light
and castles among the clouds.
i see a star waiting for a wish
and the adventures that awake in a whole new day.
With you i am born again, for through you i hear
the giggles in a babbling brook and the whisper in the wind.
i hear the crispness in a fall leaf
and the echo in "i love you."
With you i am born again, for through you i taste
the silvery tingle of a snowflake on my tongue
and all the colors in a lollypop
and i taste just how sweet life can be.
With you i am born again, for through you i feel
the devotion in a puppy's nuzzle
and comfort in the softness of a kitten.
i feel the tenderness in the tickle of a butterfly
and a celebration when mud squishes between my toes.
i feel the faith in the clasp of your tiny hand
and the warmth of security in your daddy's arms.

For want of you all I need do
is follow the little trails you leave behind.

❧❧

Oh look! A new mud puddle, never used!

❧❧

Testing his/her guardian angel.

❧❧

It's **that** smile that keeps him/her spoiled.

❧❧

All dressed up in innocence.

❧❧

You use your imagination perfectly.

❧❧

He/she is going about the business of being he/she.
(Or could use a name, animal, etc.)

Sleep Tight

Hear my footsteps across the floor
quietly to your bedroom door.
Once inside I take a peek
to see if you are fast asleep.
I cuddle up into your arms
away from all the nightly harms.

ॐ∽ॐ

Teddy Bear

Sometimes it helps a bit
to have one to tell troubles to,
everyone needs a teddy bear
for when they're feeling blue.
And when there is lots of fun about
and joy and laughter glow,
teddy's gathering memories
as one arm hangs in tow.
A teddy bear is someone special
you just never seem to outgrow.

ॐ∽ॐ

Swapping places with the tickle monster!

Mommy, I Was Wondering

Mommy, I was wondering,
does milk come from the Milky Way
and why is the golden rule golden?
Where do rainbows come from
and why do cats have whiskers?
Who is holding up the moon
and why are there cracks in the sidewalk?
Why are the trees so tall
and how big is the ocean?

Little curious one,
the milk in the sky is poured
from the angels' pitchers for little lambs
that have gone astray.
When the golden rule
is followed with good intent
hearts and faces glitter.
Rainbows are God's way of showing his love,
and the cat has whiskers to tickle you.
The moon is God's puppet
along with the sun and clouds.
The crack in the sidewalk
is where someone lost their way.
All living things grow towards God.
And the ocean is as big as my love for you.

The T-shirt
I watched you in
my t-shirt sweeping the grass
and I held my breath each time
it would tuck under your toes
and challenge you.
But you would always
bring yourself back to balance,
and that's when I knew
that you and life
were going to get along just fine.

ॐॐ

Tree Top
Serenity we search for,
sometimes found it will be,
when you're a kid
in the top of a tree.

ॐॐ

You've always been kind, but this year I think especially so.
(Could use any other attribute in place of kind.)

ॐॐ

Perfection
Ten little fingers, ten little toes,
that cute little smile under a pink nose.
You were born perfect, despite my fears,
and have grown more and more precious
throughout the years.

Little One Now Grown

My little one, now grown,
I give to you as you leave home today
three things for you to remember
and help you on your way:
Understanding, for there is reason
for all of which transpires,
it will give you wisdom
and help you gain your desires.
Hope, without it there is no future
but with it you shall see
the silver lining in every cloud,
and for every closed door, a key.
Peace, within yourself
that what you've done is right,
for it will give you confidence
and you'll shine sincerely bright.
So take these thoughts
and my never-ending love
and know that God is with you
watching from above.

My World

God chose for me to cradle within
and to guide you as you grow.
Oh breath of my breath.
Oh beat of my heart.
Oh song of my soul, I love you so.
Feeling the first flutter of life
and tasting the first teardrop to fall,
capturing the first smile straight from your heart,
and teaching you to walk from a crawl.
Look at you now, so proud am I.
My dear sweetheart, I want you to know
you've opened my eyes to a whole new world,
gave me meaning and made my life whole.

ৡৡ

Life's Lessons

When you were born, I learned
how to tiptoe again
least I wake you from your dreams.
When you were a toddler I learned
how to be a follower again,
keeping you from harm's way.
When you were a child, I learned
how to listen closely again,
to fulfill your every need.
When you were a teenager, I learned
how to set a good example again
and guide you on your way.
And now that you are grown, I've learned
how to let go and watch you fly away.

Baby

Special Child
Oh, let the world know
that on this day
tenderly, God has smiled.
Receiving grace from his perfection,
is born a special child.

કૈગ્

I was never happy to see someone cry
until the day you were born.

કૈગ્

My Newborn
I know that you were heaven sent
within these moments
when you are quietly sleeping,
holding your hands as if in prayer.

કૈગ્

I've ordered up a moon for tonight,
come slide with me on moonbeams bright.

કૈગ્

He/she rolled over and pushed Mr. Grumpy out!

Boy/Son

Soaring
Soaring high above the clouds
on the wings of a lullaby,
dreaming dreams
that make men kings,
my big blue plane and I.

ॐॐ

He wears an invisible crown
and his rod of empire rule all his treasures.

ॐॐ

You Never Know
You never know
what you will find
in that little pocket of his,
tis a riddle of treasures
only he holds the keys to.

The Box

For him, today it is a plane,
with a propeller, wings and tail.
Yesterday, it was a pirate's ship,
on the seas fighting rain and gale.
Tomorrow, it will be a train
or a spaceship high up in the sky,
but no matter where he ventures
he'll come back home by and by.

ॐ∼ॐ

The Kite

I stood so still as I watched you running
with your kite across the field
in leaps and bounds to get it off the ground—
letting a little bit of string out at a time,
until it was flying on its own.
My son, that is how I hold to you,
untying a little bit of apron string at a time
so you'll soar when you are grown.

ॐ∼ॐ

Skipping Stones

Skipping stones, catching frogs,
looking for critters under logs,
fireflies and fishing, I guess
these are the things I like best!

My Son
I've watched you fly paper planes
and kites high up in the sky
I've flown away with you
through the sparkle in your eye.

I've watched you slay the dragons
in all of your gallantry style,
and save me as your princess
as I lay draped upon your smile.

I've watched how you hit the ball
and run so fast to base,
I've found myself out of breath
for the glory in your face.

And so, in this big wide world
whatever you should become,
I will always think high of you,
my hero, my son.

Girl/Daughter

Floating
Floating high above the clouds
on the wings of a lullaby,
dreaming dreams
of pretty things,
my baby doll and I.

❧☙

The Curtsey
That's my daughter there.
She holds her dress with little pinches,
pinkie fingers pointing straight out
and dips her dress close to the shallow waves
as she curtsies to the sunset,
thanking it for the beautiful day.

<u>She's The One</u>
She's the one,
tossing the hair from her face
as she practices the art of life
in an old dress
pulled from grandma's trunk.
Oh, and the hat at one time belonged
to my mother,
and the gloves
auntie wore to church.
The heels were once in fashion,
I thought I wore them well.
Gallantly she carries the dignity
within the cloth of ones that came before her
and the shoes clap across the floor.

అ౼ళ

A smile wiggled out
as she stepped down from her chore
and went about being fancy.

Sand Castles

I can see her in the sandbox
from my kitchen sink, I gaze
upon this child so innocent
in her fantasy world she plays.
Building castles for a princess
as she is perched upon her knees,
or baking cookies, cakes and pies
with sugar crystals for a tease.
An old bowl and silver spoon
create miracles with her hand,
while yesterdays dreams
have all become
pant cuffs full of sand.

The Audience
Do the leaves of the trees
applaud in the breeze
for the rain that is to come?
Or might it be
they are rejoicing
as you dance before them
barefoot in the grass.

Growing Up
Gone are the long naps
and wobbly crawls
along with short legs
and so many falls.
You've emerged as a butterfly,
spreading your wings,
in flying colours
your spirit sings.
May your heart flutter with joy on this special day.

Gillian

I Don't Remember

I don't remember
the last time I rocked you to sleep,
but I remember your breath upon my cheek.
I don't remember
the last time I wiped prints from the wall,
but I remember thinking you could be an artist one day.
I don't remember
the last time I bundled you from the cold,
but I remember wanting to protect you in every way.
I don't remember
the last time you danced on your dad's toes,
but I remember you staring at the stars in his eyes.
I don't remember
the last time you jumped on your bed,
but I remember the delight in your smile.
I don't remember
the last time I helped you style your hair
in front of the mirror,
but I remember the reflection of love in your eyes.

ھەﻮ

My Daughter

I stand at the kitchen sink once again,
washing the same dishes we used when you were young.
I think of you and childhood days—
from the days of Cheerios on the floor each morning,
to becoming a mother,
you have bestowed me so many treasures.
The pictures you displayed on the refrigerator
have been replaced with ones from your child's hand.
Now it's their turn to measure and stir,
tug at apron strings and lick the beaters,
but we'll use the same dishes
we used when you were young.

Sister

Those hand-me-down dresses
came with lessons in the pockets.

❧❧

The Magic of a Big Sister
She will teach you how to wish upon a star
and blow magic bubbles.
She will teach you how to have a tea party
all dressed in fine hats and gloves,
She will teach you how to jump rope
and she will play with you in the sand.
She will teach you how to get ready for your first date
and when to hold hands.
And when the night seems just too long,
she will be the one who sits close by your side
and will once again teach you how to wish upon a star.

Mud Pies

I don't remember ever thanking you
for teaching me how to make mud pies
just the right kind of dirt to gather
with just the right amount of water,
how to mix it up with those big spoons,
and when it slopped on my shirt
how to smear it into fashion.
And even though that is a big sisters job
somehow you knew,
though there was no big sister to teach you
how to make mud pies just right.

❧❧

Little Sister

You were always in the way
as far as little sister's go—
I always had a hand-in-tow
always had to watch over you,
teach you things you didn't know.
I watched you fill hand-me-down dresses,
as little sisters grow.
Now I hug you as a friend,
your hand I've long let go,
but I treasure lessons in patience and love
that I learned so long ago.
You are the best there is in this whole world,
as far as little sister's go.

Remember When

I can not possibly express
the pure joy I feel in my heart
when I think of our times spent together.
It is so rare, these opportunities blessed upon us.
We weave our sorrows and troubles with unbound love,
in tears we have shared good times and bad.
These will be our memories for years to come.
The ones we share of bygone days
and the ones we weave today.
These, some of the most dearly treasured times in my life.
So many sweet memories we've yet to make,
so many sweet memories to recall,
and as our fingers lightly touch~wreathe our souls,
our eyes meet~intertwine
and nothing need be said, at all.

&~&

My Dear Sister

As I look back on all that has happened—
growing up, growing together, changing you, changing me.
The times when we dreamed together,
times when we laughed and cried together.
In all, I realize how much I miss you
and how much I truly love you.
The past is gone forever,
and our todays make the memories of tomorrow.
So, my lifelong friend, it is with all my heart
that I send you my love,
hoping that you'll always carry my smile with you,
for all that we have meant to each other
and for whatever the future may hold.

Grandparent

I love it when my grandchildren visit—
they clean the cobwebs from the corners.

ตาดดูต

Least we forget the simple things in life—
we are set right again
in the innocence of our grandchildren.

ตาดดูต

I am so young when I'm with you,
my heart flutters on wings of times long past.

Grandpa's Hands

"Grandpa, why are your hands so old
when your heart is still so young?"
"My child, my heart still has many songs
waiting to be sung.
When I was a boy,
I always wanted to be
something I never become,
and now that you have come
into my life,
I feel a new life has begun.
So let us play
and have our day
of things we would like to be,
and pay no mind
to the time
and let our hearts be free."

Friend

So often you grace my mind.

&⤳

<u>Visiting Friend</u>
I'm so glad you came to visit,
I wish you could have stayed
one more day.
I'd like to hear your voice again
and see upon your face,
one more smile.
I'd like to hold your hand again
and squeeze it just to feel
one more touch.
Our friendship is such a rare treasure,
I wish you could have stayed
one more day.

&⤳

<u>We</u>
Somewhere, in some place
wherever it may be,
here or there
we'll always share
laughter and secrets,
you and me.

Dandelions

Oh, look dear friend
how the lawn is sprinkled
with wishes to be blown.
Dare we scatter the little seeds
of hopes and dreams into summer skies
as we did when we were young?

Madison

Just Be You

I have great admiration for you,
you are a wonderful mom, wife, and friend.
I felt it the first day I met you,
but you've exceeded my expectations.
You have so much to give
to those who surround you.
I know that you have the strength,
courage, and determination
to live a life that is meaningful.
Just be you.

<u>Friend</u>

It is a rare treasure
to have a friend like you—
someone who always shows they care,
someone who always comes through,
someone who's glad to see you
whenever you drop in.
Someone who stands beside you
through the thick and thin,
someone who's smile
or just a glance it seems
conveys the message clearly,
we both know what it means.
Someone to spend the day with
and wish for nothing more—
a trip to town or just sit around
and never be a bore.
Cherished times together
are treasures in my heart
for you have brightened up my life,
and I'm glad you are that part.
Through it all
you've taught me many things,
but most of all you see
you've taught me it's okay
for me to be just me.

For a Caring Friend

Life gives us choices and challenges
and many a cross to bear.
It's so nice to know a friend is always there.
One you can laugh till you cry with,
who supports you through and through—
I know that I am truly blessed
to have such a friend in you.
You've given my life a certain finesse,
it seems right from the start.
You'll always grace a special place,
deep down inside my heart.

જ⊷৩

You strengthen my spirit and awaken my senses.

જ⊷৩

More Than

Friendship is more than just a little gesture,
it's more than having someone there.
It's more than a shared laugh, or cry, or song—
it's the embracement of a heart-felt prayer.

જ⊷৩

Birthday to a Friend

In the glory traced by timeless deeds of good,
and dear to my heart matters understood,
tis a holiday of thy true kindness and mirth,
every pleasure be thine, this day of thy birth.

Pet

I suppose he/she thinks he/she looks pretty there.

ॐ◌ॐ

Playing hide and seek with bones.

ॐ◌ॐ

Having a picnic! (carries food away from the dish.)

ॐ◌ॐ

Sleeping like a puddle on the floor.

Thank You

I will remember your kindness to me.

❧❧

Thank you for your kind and gentle manner.

Hem your blessings with my thankfulness.

❧❧

<u>Long Remembered</u>
Long remembered will be
the goodness that you have shown.
May the joy that you have given others
come round to be your own.

Acts of Kindness

Your acts of kindness
may not seem like much to you,
but they mean the world to me
for I know they're heartfelt true.

&❧

Knowing You

You are a person
who makes life easier and better
for everyone around you.
Your continual acts of thoughtfulness
and kindness brighten the day.
I appreciate you and I thank God for you.

Thank You

A simple thank you hardly seems enough
for you didn't have to be so caring,
or listen to me complain.
You didn't have to welcome me
or comfort me in pain.
You didn't have to wish me well,
or go that extra mile,
but you did it all so naturally,
restoring for me, my smile.

༶∾᠙

Gift of Time

I thank you for the precious gift of time
that you have spent with me.
Cherished in my heart
and in my memory
it shall ever be.

Miscellaneous

Practice

Practice

Practice

ॐ❦

We all must learn to curtsey least we meet the Queen.

ॐ❦

My bestest one!

ॐ❦

We can just pretend it's _____.
(Day of week, type of food, animal, toy, weather, etc.)

Introduce yourself to the new day.

꙳꙳

Off to find the riddle of the day.

꙳꙳

Off to find the remainder of the day.

꙳꙳

Off to another place in time.

꙳꙳

In the distance, life is rushing to find its day.

Karmin

Hugs and kisses and happy day wishes.

❧❦

Grumbles and groans.

❧❦

I am not stumbling . . .
I am dancing with the fairies.

❧❦

I didn't fall . . .
I just decided to dust the floor.

❧❦

As we walk this path together and share our lives.
Let's kick up a little dust!

❧❦

Always be open to change
for it is there where the true adventure begins.

❧❦

If I should ever fall from grace,
I hope I land in your arms.

❧❦

A big loving heart and wide-eyed smiles
with laughter that comes in all kinds of styles.

You are the kind of person that sees the beauty
in a flower growing in the poorest of soil.

☙❧

For all my years you will be in my thoughts.

☙❧

Each day I pray that the angels
will tickle you with their blessings.

☙❧

I wish you blessed
with memories dressed
in laughter, love, and pride.

☙❧

May the gentle breezes of today
encircle you with joy and gladness.

☙❧

May thee tarry today
within a garden of memories
and plenty be thy cherished blooms.

☙❧

The morning light tiptoes through the room
as might an angel would, blessing all within.

<u>Tea Time</u>
I've captured nature's sugar
and the tea is plenty hot,
it would be so pleasing
if you could share with me a pot.

❧❦

The subject of _____ keeps us in chorus for hours.

❧❦

<u>Chicken Soup</u>
Henny Penny flew the coop,
she was only trying to avoid the soup,
but as she flew to and fro
she flapped her wings
she scratched with her toe . . .
stars right out of the blue.
They all fell down into the stew
and that is how soup came to be
a chicken and stars out on a spree!

❧❦

Within quiet repose
is found our most divine rewards.

Full Measure
Although you stand
shorter than I
and your age
is a bit younger than mine,
you stand so very tall in my eyes.

&ra&

I seem to stand taller when I'm with you.

&ra&

Do not let me linger in time
to be less than I can be.

&ra&

I will try to stand where you can be proud.

&ra&

The American Flag
As each day's dawn echoes new light
cast upon colors of blue, red and white,
and as the wind finds its lengths to unfold
the stories of wartime and heroes are told.
Proudly we wave, united and free,
the American Flag for all to see.

Aging

<u>Birthday Wishes</u>
Laughter, smiles, friends to share
and all the happiness you find there,
is just what we wish for your birthday!

෨෧

<u>Young At Heart</u>
Birthdays come
and birthdays go
and for all the candles
you may have wished upon
I just really want you to know
that you have always been,
and will forever be,
especially beautiful in my eyes
and young at heart to me.

෨෧

Seasons have changed and I am growing still.

෨෧

I'm beginning to wear an old woman's face.

෨෧

My forehead is beginning to drip off my cheeks,
some people call them jowls.

Memories

If not for the journaling . . .
Oh the memories time would have taken from me.

৵৽

I've dusted my memories and polished the good ones.

৵৽

There's nothing like bathing in a good memory.

৵৽

There are moments in our lives that will never be forgotten
and places in our hearts that will always be cherished.

৵৽

When was it last so long ago the gentle song you sang to me
now graciously posed in memory?

৵৽

Your voice wraps around my soul, and carries me home again.

The Open Door

Remember how we used to race
to the front door after getting off the school bus?
Your laughter teased the wind as it swept past me.
Your leaps were my two steps
and you always got there first.
But you left the door open for me.
And yet still, you always leave a door open for me.

<u>I Remember</u>
I remember . . .
waking up on cold, crisp mornings,
my dad sitting in the dark
drinking his coffee
while soft music flowed from the radio.
I remember . . .
trying to beat the chill
as I ran with clothes in hand
to the warmest place in the house—
behind the curtain that held the hot air
as it escaped from the hole in the floor.
I remember . . .
the frost on the mailbox
looking so inviting
that I could not resist taking a lick
only to be hopelessly stuck,
and waiting for a glass of water
to be brought from the house to free me,
thinking never again
would I give so easily to temptation.
I remember . . .
stretching out on the living room floor
letting the sun's warmth
fill me on a Sunday afternoon,
thinking about all of my childhood
and all the things
I would want to remember.

Death

She

She must have been very special
for God to take her hand
and lead her into heaven
into the Promised Land.
And though we will miss her sweet smile
and her special ways,
we know that one day there will be
many brighter days.
So let's remember her
and the fun times we did share,
and know that deep within our hearts
she will always be there.

ॐ

Moonbeams

I ride away on moonbeams bright
passing through the still of night,
dancing across the land below
kissing drifts of new fallen snow.
Yet in the early morning's light
no trail of me remains in sight,
my golden footsteps leave no trace,
my kiss swept away by wind's embrace.

Mourning
We sit quietly side by side and mourn our loss.
We search for comfort through tear filled eyes and sigh
as we feel a hand from heaven gently lifting our hearts.

འ⁓⁓

Graveside
Dear _____
I visited your grave today.
I cleaned the leaves away
that had gathered around your headstone.
And as I tided up,
I listened to the noises that echo around you—
The leaves, still clinging to the trees
were whispering to themselves,
a bird in song, celebrating the day.
So peaceful here.

Gardening/Nature

Take time to grow in your garden.

ৡৼ

A soul just seems to rest a bit closer to God,
on bended knee, tending plants, fingers deep in sod.

ৡৼ

Come for coffee, come for tea.
Come see my garden, come to see me!

Melanie

Four Seasons Garden
(verse for a card with gift
of a picture, shirt, etc. with flowers on it)

I've planted for you a garden,
I've tended with such care
in hopes that you may come to find
some peace and respite there.
It is a carefree garden
you'll never have to weed,
you'll never have to mend a fence
or sow a single seed.
Come and visit anytime,
early spring through winters end,
and you'll find a bouquet waiting for you
time and time again.

🔖

The sun came skipping through the wood
playing hide and seek with all the creatures there.

🔖

We left the mountains standing proudly against the sky.

🔖

God's Miracles
From the first bud in springtime
to the last bloom in fall,
I'm amazed at God's miracles
I love them all.

Seasons

Spring

The snow tickled the toes of my daffodils
this morning as it melted away.

❧❦

Spring is peeking around the corner in fits and starts.

❧❦

The Angel's Petticoat
What angel's petticoat is whispering in the wood
amongst the flowering dogwood there?
Tis the angel of Springtime
enticing the new leaves to open,
and its delicate petals to blush.

❧❦

The branches are pouring out little green leaves
to take their place in the big world.

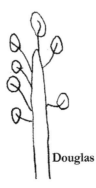

Douglas

Summer

Soon the Queen Anne's Lace
will open and sit atop the grasses
as plates upon a table.

సౌళ

Next Year's Garden
The flowers will soon sneeze
and its seeds will sail upon the wind
finding a perfect place to land
and next year's garden will begin.

Fall

<u>Fall Leaves</u>
The reds and golds
play tag
as they swirl in circles
across the ground.

ॐॐ

The campfire begs to be watched
as it crackles in the evening air.

The Little Leaf

Off the branch, the little leaf falls
and takes a dip as it flies through the air
spinning,

 floating, off somewhere
joining others on the ground
as if it were
dancing,

 tumbling all around.
And just as it seems to rest a bit
the wind begs it,

 "Do not quit.

   Come fly with me,

   come explore.

   We'll have fun just like before!"
But the leaves whisper,
"Shhh, it's time for sleep,
for soon a blanket of snow will creep
upon the land for tis all in the plan
of the one who is stronger than thee."

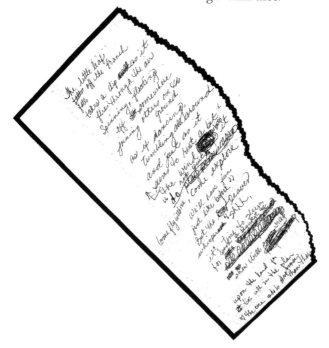

Winter

<u>Snowman</u>
A nice tall snowman
with a high, high hat,
a big black rim
all nice and flat!
With two coal eyes
and a carrot nose,
and a long, long scarf
for when the wind blows!
With two stick arms
quite long and dense
a place to rest
for his feathered friends.

ॐ✦

<u>Man Made of Snow</u>
All of a heap
he's lumpy and plump
and his scarf in the wind doth blow . . .
In a round-about way
he's fluffy inside . . .
Alas! He's our man made of snow!

Holidays

Valentine's Day

Happy Valentine's Day
So here we are at last, my love, just the two of us.
And in a way you could say that we are beginning
our lives together again, except . . .
I know how it feels when you hold me
and I know the look of love in your eyes.
I know the tenderness of your sweet touch
and the warmth in your kiss of good-bye.
I know how it feels when you wait for me
in anxious anticipation, and how your heart
just seems to rest a bit upon our togetherness again.
You have been my anchor when I have rocked about
uncertain of my way. You have been my sail
leading me to places I never dared dream.
You are on this day, and everyday,
My Valentine

Halloween

<u>Witches Brew</u>
Light of moon
dark of day
follow the stars
to guide your way.
Choose Staghorn sumac
and chanterelle,
pot them up
and mix them well.
With moss and bark
from a fallen tree,
do as I've done
and let it be.
Chant the spell
and it be done
as sure as the spider's
web be spun.

<u>All Hallows Eve</u>

m**A**king haste
fading **L**ight
Little goblins

run in frig**H**t
witches c**A**ckle
b**L**ack cats stare
bones ratt**L**e
jack-**O**-lanterns glare
spirits **W**horl
Spooks in sight

the masquerad**E**
Vanishes
com**E** morning light

Christmas

No Peeking
Tho' tis the holiday
of hiding and seeking,
when wishes and packages
tease thee to sneaking,
don't open till Christmas,
remember ~ no peeking!

ક>ન્જ

Merry Christmas
Tinsel, candles,
peppermint stick,
mistletoe, packages
and Ol' Saint Nick!
Merry Christmas!

ક>ન્જ

Christmas hug, warm and snug!

ક>ન્જ

Wreathed smiles, presents in piles,
amongst my wishes merry.

ક>ન્જ

Christmas folly, spirits jolly, every joy be thine.

ક>ન્જ

Midst the swirls of winter snow, bright be thy Christmas.

Blessed sight, Christmas white.
Angel of peace be with thee.

❧❧

From whence the herald angels fly
and host good will to you and I—
blessed be thy Christmas.

❧❧

In woodland walks amongst the pine
where soul and nature's song entwine,
may the peace found there-in be thine
this holiday season.

❧❧

Recall the warmth of yuletides past
nestled in your heart
and you'll embrace my dearest wishes
for you this blessed season.

❧❧

In the silence of the snow
reflecting moments of long ago,
may you find drifts of pleasant memories
this holiday season.

❧❧

Nestled among the packages and piles
nod's and beck's and little wreathed smiles,
angels weave tidings of joy and delight.
Blessed season to you, thy Christmas be bright.

<u>Season's Greetings</u>
Flickering candles, Christmas aglow,
the essence of cinnamon stick, ginger and clove.
Heartfelt hugs and wishes to sow,
packages adorned with ribbon and bow
examined by children on bended knee,
popcorn strung upon the tree,
twinkling lights for all to see,
Season's Greetings to you from me.